Watch Me Read and Draw

Noah's Ark

Illustrated by Jannie Ho

How to Use This Book

This book is special because it blends two things together that kids love. In this book, you get to read AND draw!
Inside, you will find:

A fun story to read

11 step-by-step drawing lessons

A flip-out drawing pad with guidelines

Once the Earth was dry, Noah and his family helped the animals out of the ark.

Draw the zebra!

When you finish your drawing, place the aardvark sticker on the opposite page!

Add the zebra's tail, ears, and face. Finish your drawing with its stripes and mane.

Stickers to complete each scene

A scene to make your own

Draw your own scene here, and add some stickers too!

Here is the best way to enjoy this book:
Sit down with an adult and grab
your drawing supplies.

Read through the story together,
following along with each lesson
on the flip-out drawing pad.

Add the zebra's tail, ears, and face.
Finish your drawing with its stripes and mane.

When you complete a
lesson, add a sticker to
the scene. Good job!

Once the Earth was dry, Noah
and his family helped the
animals out of the ark.

Draw your own scene here, and add some stickers too!

Draw your own scene at
the end with the characters
you have learned, and add
some stickers.

Great work!
Now you can draw the
story of Noah's Ark
any time you want!

Noah was a good man.
But not everyone on Earth
was good like Noah.

God decided to wash the Earth clean with a great flood. God told Noah to build an ark and gather two of every living creature on Earth.

Draw Noah!

When you finish your drawing, place the squirrel sticker on the opposite page!

Noah and his sons built the ark to keep all of the animals safe during the flood.

Draw the ark!

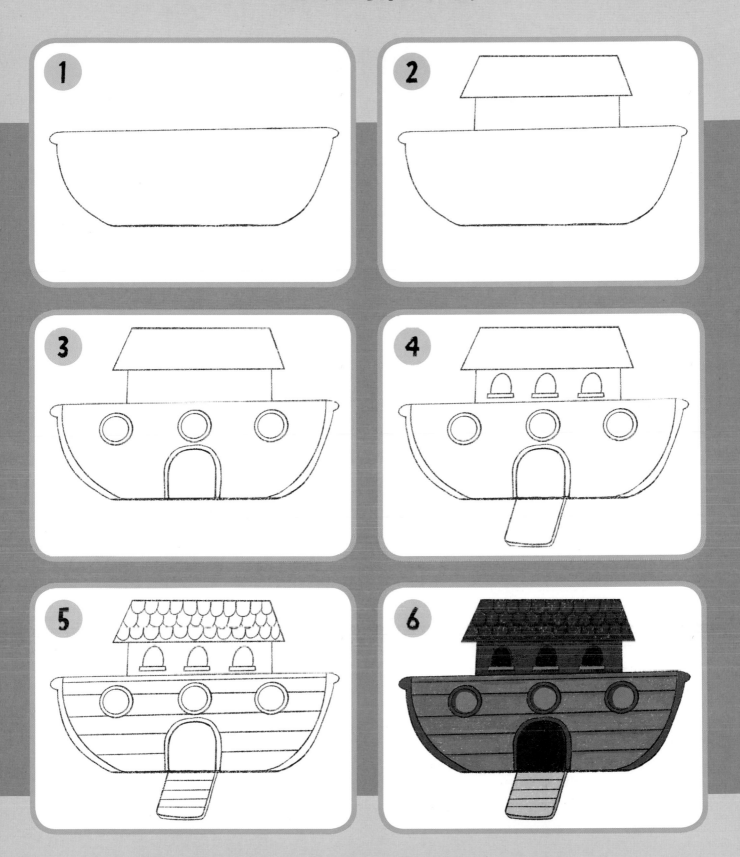

When you finish your drawing, place the bird sticker on the opposite page!

Animals of all sizes began to fill
the ark, from the birds of the sky
to the creatures of the Earth—
even the smallest mouse!

Draw the mouse!

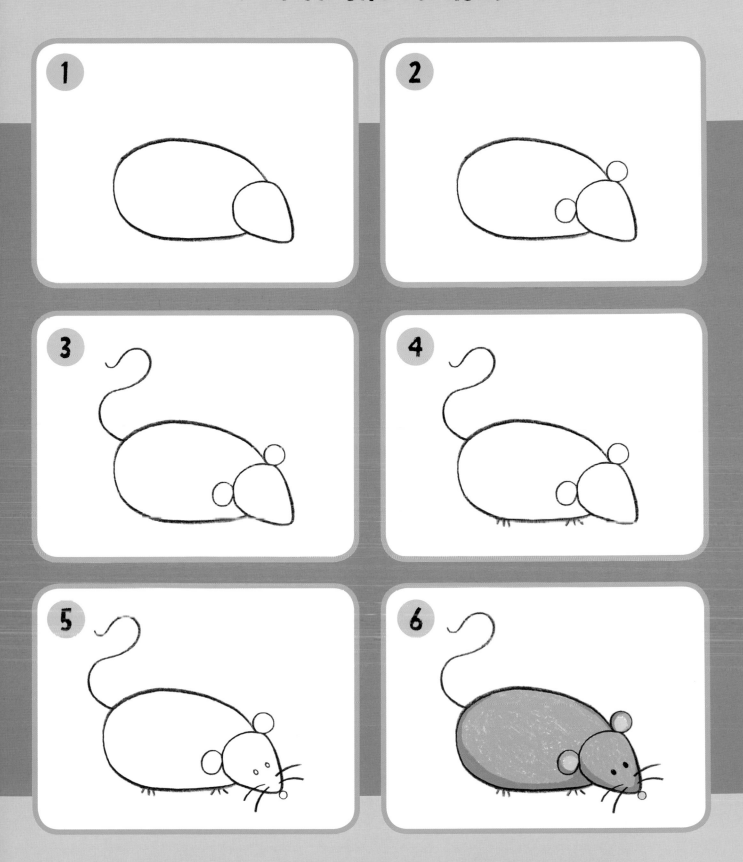

When you finish your drawing, place the
sheep sticker on the opposite page!

Noah and his family gathered the animals, two by two, and helped them onto the ark.

Draw the giraffe!

When you finish your drawing, place the
lizard sticker on the opposite page!

Just as the last animal crept
onto the ark, it began to rain.

Draw the sloth!

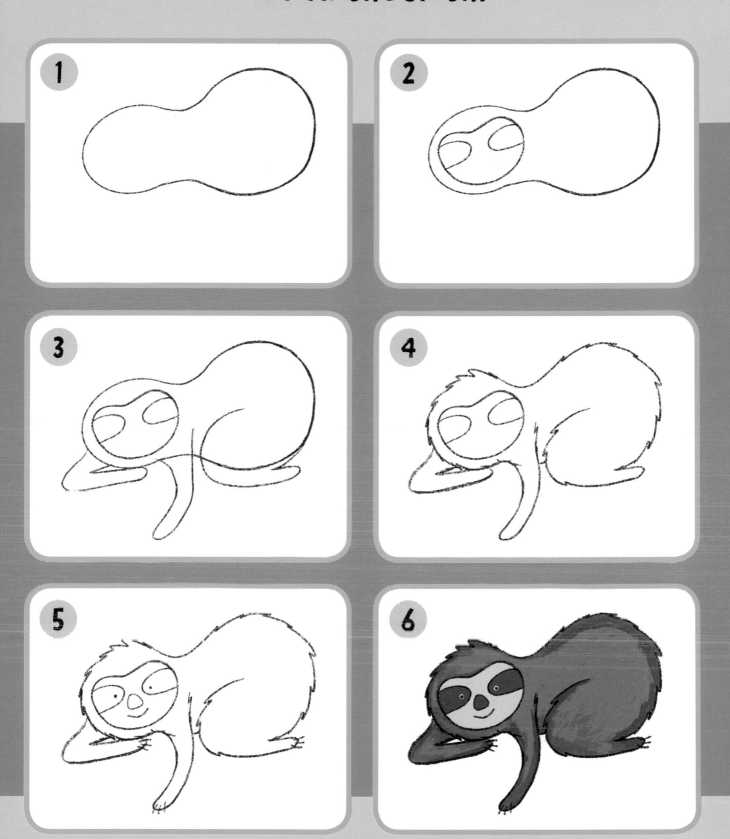

When you finish your drawing, place the
mice sticker on the opposite page!

It rained for forty days and forty nights. Noah comforted the animals and told them that God would take care of them.

Draw the squirrel!

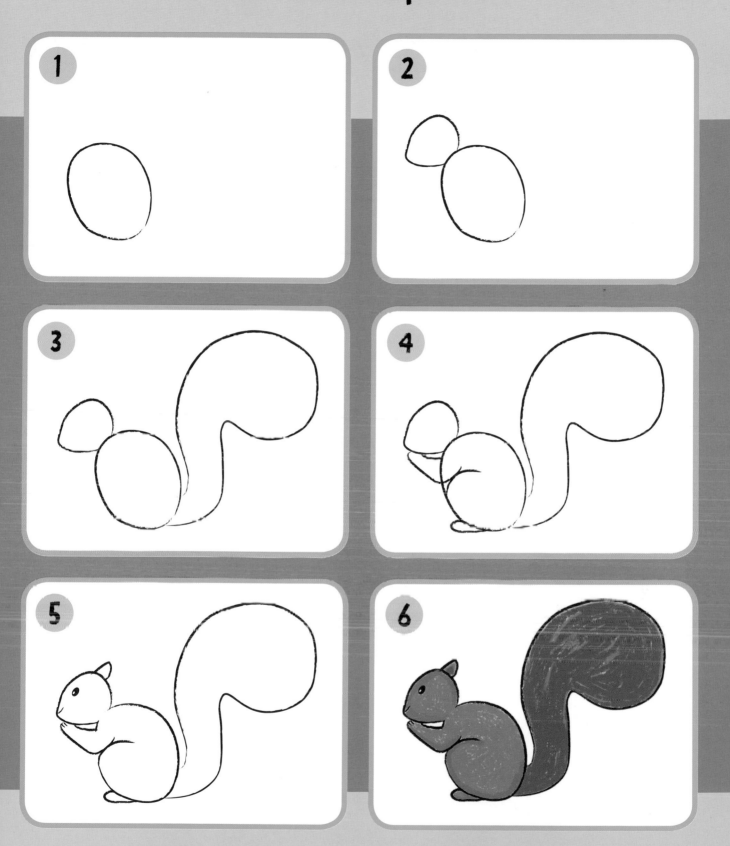

When you finish your drawing, place the
sloth sticker on the opposite page!

The flood covered the Earth for 150 days, but Noah's family and the animals were safe in the ark, just as God had said.

Draw the whale!

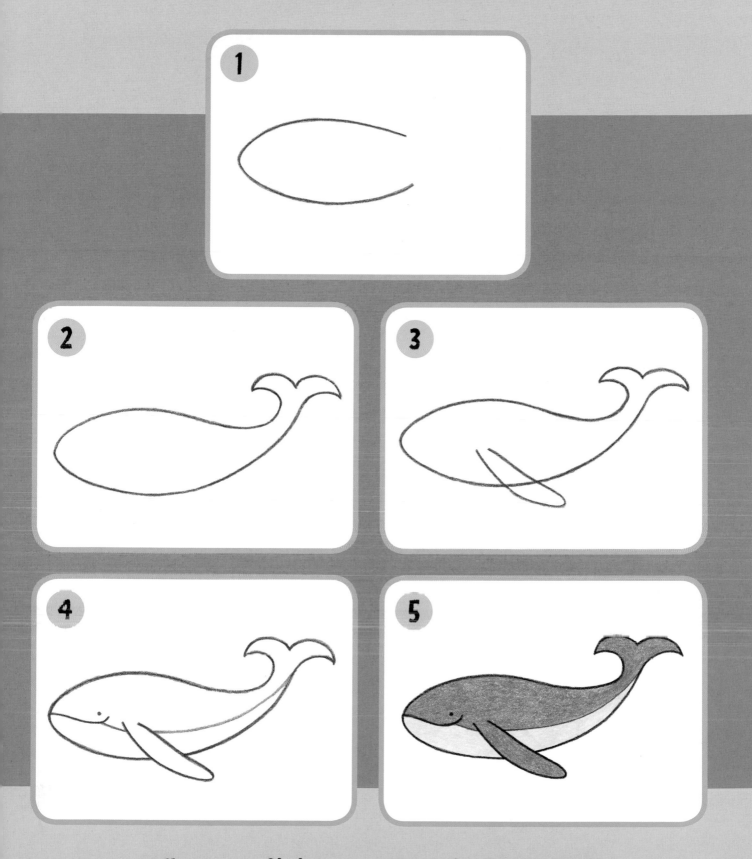

When you finish your drawing, place the fish sticker on the opposite page!

A wind blew, the water went down,
and the ark landed on a mountaintop.
Noah and all of the animals were happy.

Draw the lion!

When you finish your drawing, place the flamingos sticker on the opposite page!

Noah sent out a dove to search for more dry land.
One day, she didn't come back.
She must have found a place to land!

Draw the dove!

When you finish your drawing, place the giraffe sticker on the opposite page!

Once the Earth was dry, Noah and his family helped the animals out of the ark.

Draw the zebra!

When you finish your drawing, place the
aardvark sticker on the opposite page!

Noah and his family
thanked God for saving them.
God created a rainbow in the sky
as a sign of His promise to never
again flood the Earth.

Draw the rainbow!

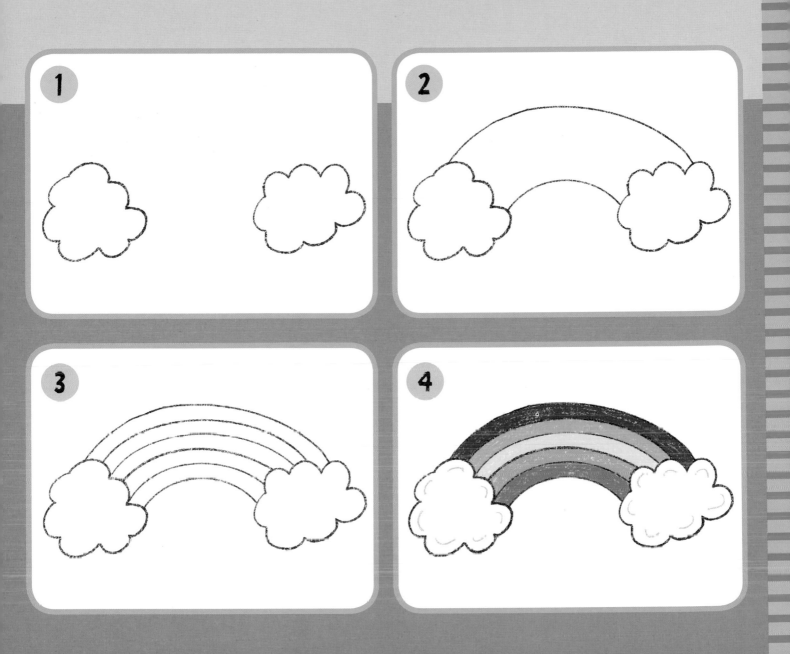

When you finish your drawing, place the
lion sticker on the opposite page!

The End

Draw your own scene here, and add some stickers too!

Great job!

_____
Print your name here

Congratulations on completing the story. Keep drawing and reading!

Finish-the-Scene Stickers

Draw Noah's eyes, nose, and mouth.
Don't forget the details on his clothes.

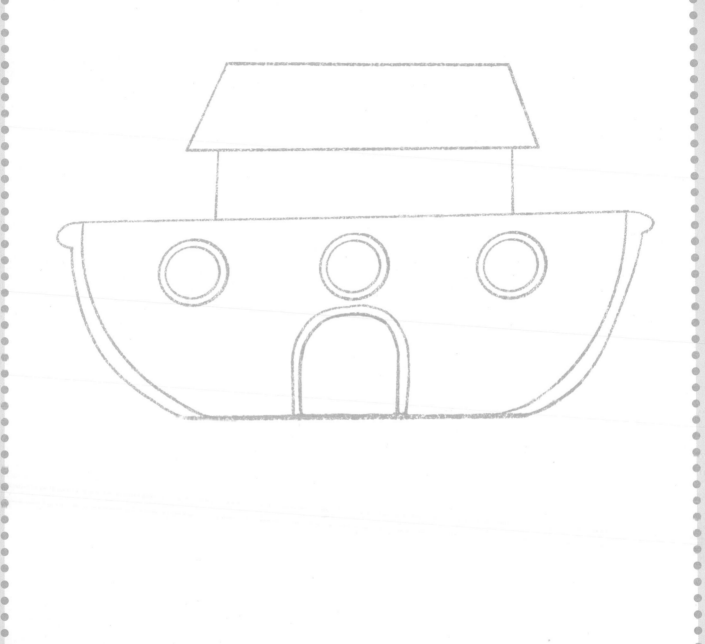

Add the details on the ark, such as the planks of wood, windows, and roof tiles.

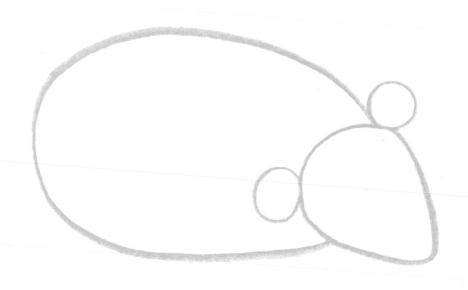

Draw the mouse's tail.
Then add its eyes and nose.

Draw the giraffe's tail, ears, and horns.
Add the mane, spotted pattern, face, and hooves.

Draw the sloth's eyes, nose, and long claws.
Don't forget its smile!

Add the squirrel's arms and legs.
Finish your drawing with its ears and face.

Draw the whale's fin. Make a line for the belly.
Then add the mouth and eye.

Draw the lion's legs. Add its toes and tail.
Then draw the eyes, nose, and smile.

Add the dove's eye, beak, and feet.
Draw more of the wing feathers too.

Add the zebra's tail, ears, and face.
Finish your drawing with its stripes and mane.

Make sure you have five stripes on your rainbow.

You can draw your own scene here.

You can draw your own scene here.

Woman's Guide
to Spiritual Wellness

A Personal Study
of Colossians

Rhonda Harrington Kelley

New Hope Publishers
Birmingham, Alabama

New Hope® Publishers
P. O. Box 12065
Birmingham, AL 35202-2065

© 1998 by New Hope® Publishers
First printing 1998
Printed in the United States of America

Unless otherwise indicated, all Scripture quotations are taken from the New King James Version. © 1982 by Thomas Nelson, Inc. Used by permission. All rights reserved.

Cover design by Pam Moore

ISBN: 1-56309-252-2